SINCERITY OF SUNLIGHT

SINCERITY OF SUNLIGHT

A BOOK OF INSPIRATION

JAIYA JOHN

Soul Water Rising

Camarillo, California

Printed in the United States of America

Soul Water Rising
Camarillo, California
http://www.soulwater.org

Library of Congress Control Number: 2017903184
ISBN 978-0-9916401-9-5

First Soul Water Rising Edition, Softcover: 2017
Second printing: 2021

Inspiration / affirmation / spirituality

Editors: Jacqueline V. Carter
                                           Kent W. Mortensen

Cover & Interior Design: Jaiya John
Cover Photo: Jaiya John

Unearth your luminous soul.

Also by Jaiya John

Freedom: Medicine Words for Your Brave Revolution
Daughter Drink This Water
Calm: Inspiration for a Possible Life
Fresh Peace: Daily Blossoming of the Soul
Your Caring Heart: Renewal for Helping Professionals and
Systems
Clear Moon Tribe
The Day Jumoke Found His Name
Legendary: A Tribute to Those Who Honorably Serve Devalued
Children
Beautiful: A Poetic Celebration of Displaced Children
Reflection Pond: Nurturing Wholeness in Displaced
Children
Habanero Love: A Poem of Sacred Passion
Father to Son: Ode to Black Boys
Lyric of Silence: A Poetic Telling of the Human Soul Journey
Black Baby White Hands: A View from the Crib

WELCOME

It is good to see you here, dear one. This book is a peace offering. I hope you will take a full, free, true breath, and settle in for a precious moment of peace. That you will open up and be still long enough for these words to enter you and sink into the soil of your being. I hope you will make these words medicine seeds that you water with gentle attention, so they may sprout and break through the crusted ground of your weary consciousness. If you do this, these words may do more than inspire you. They may feed you as you choose to live and Love as the sincerity of sunlight. This is what happens when we hold our habitual idea of life up to the Light of Truth. Its uncompromising radiance burns away the illusions that cause our suffering. What grows up from the after-burn is new life. The true life we are born to live. Have you seen what the sun has done to this world? You, my friend, can do that, too.

Look what the sun did to the world as it rose this morning. It did not hold back its Love, and now everything glows miraculously. As all things in the Web of Life are related, you too must hold the power of the sun. Rise today. Don't just move through your moments like a stick in a stream. Love like the sun. Make the whole world glow and blush. Your reward will be a day full of sunrises shining wonderfully back at you.

Hope is an heirloom passed down the generations of souls in morning / mourning. A treasure shared between those on the simultaneous shores of pain and paradise. Hope whispers a secret of how living things remain alive. Hope sings. Sings in notes tuned to the range of human despair and defiance. Hope is a rope you swing over the canyon chasm of fear, swinging above the murky sediment of doubt settled at the bottom of the polluted river of pessimism. When you release your tears to flow down your cheeks, those tears are hope messengers on their way to your heart. They have something fresh and fragrant to deliver.

Hope is a resurrected Light. Behold as it reanimates what has surrendered to thoughts of doom. It is that impossible breeze through the wide window that puts to sleep the candle flame, then returns to bring the burning back to life. Hope is a reunion with the surreal peace ever inside your divine nature. It brings you to that palace, opens the door, hosts your visit, serves you nourishment, grants you a soft bed and fresh sheets for supernatural rest. Hope is a home.

Hope is a dawn, a dusk, a turning. Hope lives in your yearning.

Hope speaks in the dialect of Promise. The stories it tells are of legends and mystical happenings that reason says could not have happened. Hope is not reasonable. Not seasonable. Hope is an everlasting atmosphere. Hope is untamed, incorrigible, feral, and free. Hope cannot be discouraged. It is a titanic waterfall that drowns your discouragement, sweeps you to the ocean where breeds of hopeful things migrate in the deep decadence of being. Hope bleeds. Its sanguine outflow expels from you the accumulated toxins from your lifetime. Hope expunges the long record of your personal harms. Hope is not a judge or jury but a trail guide pointing you toward the place of your reckoning. Hope places your duty in your hands and sets you off to shape that clay.

Hope purifies your persona. Weaves peace through your dense jungle of worries. Hope is a medicine wheel. It offers you the four directions, four teachers, four elements, and the ancestral assignment: *Care for each other no matter what.* Hope is dreamcatcher. It snares your skepticism, burns it in the blinding brightness of Grace. Hope delivers to you the sacred dreams that hold your valleys of tall grass, clear water, and circles of ceremony between living things.

Hope rises. It is lighter than your lightest ideas. Just when you believe Hope has died, Hope rises again. Even in the crevasses of your pain and loneliness, Hope rises. In your private self-disgust and disbelief in this life, Hope lives there, too. Lifting as a mist, spreading its gospel until that scripture becomes the entire sky. Hope burns your sacred plants. Hope is the plant, the flame, the burning, the smoke, the fragrance, the spirit, the clearing. Hope is a cathedral, glistening through the stained glass, vibrating in the bellows, reaching for the arches, polishing the wood for prayer.

Hope is in the silence you suffer and savor. Hope laces your laughter with a friend. Hope musters your courage to touch what in this world you feel dearly needs to change. Hope scatters fertile seeds in its wind. Hope's long fingers plant in the soil. Hope is a water feeding the sprout. Hope is the sunlight to greet what breaks through from the crust of ground. Hope is what rises and fattens and blooms into fruit. Hope is in your biting, your eating, your robust renewal.

Hope is your awakening when you pause long enough, are hit hard enough, are awed deeply enough, lose enough, are emptied enough, rendered and shuddered to the bone. Hope opens your eyes. Dilates your heart. Suffuses your breath and body with the oxygen of determination.

Hope is the gift Grace offers you today. A flower that will not wilt. All that is Love is Loving you in this present breath. All that you are feeling is medicine for our great healing. And though you may feel that your ordered life has fallen, be comforted in this ascendant Truth: Hope is a Miracle. Already risen. In you.

You may not remember this, but many years ago you felt something move through you that left you weeping. You thought to yourself: *This is the happiest I have ever been*. That joy never left you. It is a dormant seed, waiting and well. With care, you can raise joy's flower into the sunlight of your life, and keep it there.

We are created to live in the territory of the soul. Instead we wander in the abyss of the mind, pained with a yearning for the soul. We can solve our paradox. Devotion to anything results in becoming our devotion. When you find yourself sweetened and in the soul's paradise, record how it feels and how you got there. And when you are lost and wandering through an overgrowth of thoughts, simply take note. Smile and release. Begin your soulfulness again.

Two desires live in us. One, of the soul, and one caused by fear. Fear-based desire only cares to escape the feeling of fear, regardless of the harm to which this fleeing leads. Soul fire burns for Love's bidding, regardless of any discomfort. Learn to live a life of soul desire. The beauty of which will set this world afire. And a new world will rise. And you shall taste the sweet spice of fulfillment. We are speaking here of fire keeping. The fire you tend to, thrives. The other cools down to weakened embers. Stay by your soul fire. It will warm even the idea of you.

Life is a flower, petals open to your advances, nectar awaiting your appetite. And you are a hummingbird, a butterfly. Do what you were born to do. Come get this Amazing Grace.

Life has countless rhythms, many of which are rivers carrying us away from our true self. Only when we are in rhythm with the sweet flagrancy of Love, do we dance to the music of our soul, and discover the luminescent garden that the sages call...

Being Alive.

If it were not for Love, you would have nowhere to pour your soul waters. No basin, no riverbed, no waterfall. Were it not for Love, you would have no height from which to drop your tears. No tree, no cloud, no atmosphere. Were it not for Love, you would have no ground from which to rise. No earth, no garden, no valley. If it were not for Love, your glory would have no way of existing in this world. And this glorious world would have no way of existing in you.

Hallelujah.

For there is Love.

The way we move through each day is a deeply ingrained choice, repeated over years. It is a choice that in our mind has become simply *the way life is*, or, *the way I am*. We fail to realize we are living out a series of daily and moment-to-moment choices. Habit should not be confused with a *Law of Life*. No law exists that forces us to be of a certain mood, spirit, emotion, attitude, or perspective. We own that choice. Which we can forge into a new habit. If we choose. You are moving through your day right now in the way of your choice. May that choice be in a direction that warms all souls.

Including, most of all, your own.

Today is a blank sheet of paper awaiting the perfect inspiration of your soul, which is always perfect. Write something from your soul. Be assured, it will be perfect. Stay in your soul lane. Avoid the world where your drafting becomes imitative, flawed, insincere. Imprint these hours with your lush script of inner truth. Forge a story that speaks in a clear voice, decided upon itself, and devoted to freedom. Erase all the false alphabets you have acquired. Soul writing and living require a nakedness that blushes the sky.

A man says to his friend, "I am having pain in my uterus."

His friend, startled, replies, "You do not have a uterus."

The man says, "Then I really do have a problem."

Bless us, for it seems that so often we create in our minds places to experience, store, and preserve our pain, even when those places are not real. We create reasons, associations, reminders, points of blame, habits, patterns, fallback and default attitude settings, and on and on. All of these are containers in which we keep and even increase pain that originally existed in a specific moment, from a very specific cause.

What if we erased these storage bins? How would our pain behave then? Perhaps like morning mist, marine layer, or passing clouds... lightly lifting away from us, in a natural, gradual manner. Eventually revealing the light of day.

Pain is not ours to keep. It is only ours to make meaning of as it goes along its way. With pain, we try to domesticate a wild thing. Letting this wildness go is another way of allowing Light to come inside our soul.

Funny thing about rain barrels. They work. The design is simple enough: *A vessel that is wide open*. It fills with sky water, which we then use to bless our family's thirst and cleansing needs. And to bless our plants and animals. Something pure falls from the sky, and a rain barrel harvests it. All because it is wide open.

We stand in a glorious skyfall called *being alive*. When a rain of blessings happens, and it is always happening, may you be fortunate enough to be wide open. Then you too can be a barrel into which the thirsty dip their daily cups and drink.

A healthy culture socializes us into wellness. An unhealthy culture socializes us into unwellness. Ultimately, we are being shaped. The question is: *In whose hands*? We have been given the ability to discern what is good for us, and what is not. In choosing whose hands shall shape us, we craft the quality of our life. First, we might pause and ask whether we should assume that our culture, and what is celebrated and encouraged inside of it, is a hand by which we wish to be shaped. If we wish to be shaped and forged into a Divine life, then perhaps we should choose Divine hands.

Your life today offers an endless array of Divine choices. From the way nature behaves, to compassionate examples of being human. And then there are those choices offered by a flawed culture that may or may not be so healthful. Smorgasbords and buffets are wonderful, so long as we choose the true delicacies on display.

When a baby cries, we fill with a primal desire to treat and end its suffering.

When the world cries out, we often fill with a sense of being overwhelmed, as though the suffering is too great for us to even consider.

And when our own heart cries out, we are likely to fill with a notion that our personal suffering is not worthy of our rapt attention.

A healthy mother will respond to her baby's cry without considering whether she is maternally capable, and without regard to whether her baby's suffering is worthy of attention. A healthy mother will simply treat the suffering.

Somewhere in us is an instinct waiting to be tapped wide open. An instinct that causes us to treat all suffering, compassionately. Suffering of a baby, of the world, and in ourselves. We are each a river, contending with boulders in our water, blessed with a force of compassionate flow. We are healers. You are among the truest of these. Let it flow.

A meadow lives inside of us. When we are in this meadow we can see our life clearly: all the contours and topography, the rise and fall of the hills, the shadows and light, streams and rivers, sky and horizon. We can see clearly the place from which we have come, our location at the moment, and where we are headed. We can see clearly, feel clearly, and understand clearly. When we are in this meadow, we have the Peace and assurance that clarity brings.

The key is for us to get to this meadow. And remain there. We arrive by learning to be still, to fill with the pure Grace of this life and nature, and to release our minds from worry and distraction. We arrive by learning to be in harmony with all that is. We remain in the meadow by falling in Love with what it is like to be there.

Be a Lover of the meadow where you find clarity. Memorize its location. Create a path. Put your roots down there.

This morning, dip your palms into the clear water and drink Truth. Wash your wonderful face in Truth. Fear accumulations have wrapped a haze of illusion around you and everyone. This morning, wash your spirit clean. Come back to Truth: *the healing nature of Love*. The union of Creation. The way all things flow inseparably. Grace making sure that you are going to be all right. Beauty holding sermons inside every shaft of sun, caress of breeze, stillness and silence. Pain's flowering into a useful fruit. Forgiveness shattering the prisons in which we languish. The way our deep and mindful breath is like a masseuse, releasing our various parts from tension, aligning them as a caring and gifted chiropractor would. The way your life turns and billows, a luminous blanket in sunlight, drifting so wonder-fully.

Remember Ahab and his quest for the white whale? Obsession was not so good for Ahab. Obsession itself, though, is not always a harmful thing. Flowers and plants obsess over sunshine. Animals in autumn obsess over storing food, in dens or in the fat of their body. Worshipers obsess over God. Parents over the wellbeing of their children. Musicians over music and the glory of sound and word.

And then there are those who obsess over Peace. For better or for worse, they immerse their mind and being into Peaceful waters. One thing we do know is that these obsessive ones seem to be filled with the object of their obsession. They emanate it. In this way, we are what we obsess.

If it is true that we have a human tendency toward obsession, at least let us pick something to be consumed by that brightens and eases our day, and that lets us give the world a Loving kiss.

If we go to nature to find peace, it is natural to assume that nature holds the nature of peace. Something about a lake contains peace, or else we would not find peace there. Looking into a lake, keeping it company, we see and feel its calm, relaxed state. This can be a clue to the state we should be in, if we too want to contain peace: A lake lets go. Birds arrive and leave freely. Sky moves over unobstructed. And a lake's waters move in rhythm with sun and moon, day and night. *Calm, relaxed, released, in rhythm*. If we practice to become these things, maybe others will come to us to find their lake of peace.

Somewhere between earth and moon is a place where the gravity of one is in harmony with the gravity of the other. *A place of mutual attraction.* This is what holds the universe in place. You have your own gravity, drawing all things to you. Walk in beauty now so that you may be pulled into the atmosphere of all that blesses and heals you, and gives you joy. Find these places of harmonistic convergence, where what you want wants you equally. Find these places where gravity's pull is mutual, natural, at ease. Walk close to the ocean, feel your spirit pull at those waters, just as those waters pull at you. Move through this world finding places where what you need needs what you are. Here you will find balance, and the wonder of harmonious bliss.

What you see when you look in the mirror is only mist obscuring your true essence. Look into the mirror of Sacredness. What you see there will take away doubt of your beauty and worth. We walk in this world under cover of mask and clothing: face and body. These cloaks eclipse our soul and highlight a sense of separateness. And so we suffer against ourselves and with each other. Look into the mirror of Sacredness, a truth gleaming on every surface, from every line and contour. What you will find is not vanity, but tonic for perception's insanity. You will find the face and form of your authentic value. Your everlasting Grace.

Soul burrows out through your eyes, until you feel strong emotion. Then it changes its body to water and flows down your face. This is the soul releasing itself, and making itself known. Tears are not the flag bearers of suffering in the parade of life. They are the pure dance the soul does when it is moved so deeply it cannot help but flood the world into being more soulful. A prairie dog leaves its burrow and sniffs the air when it is moved to be out in the world. Soul burrows out through your eyes, until it is moved to immerse this world in soulfulness. Let your life be a wide open prairie, full of breeze and light, inviting your soul to make many Divine appearances.

In life, stones and silt accumulate in the riverbed of the soul. Always be dredging, clearing. Wheat is always growing in the form of blessing inside of every moment. Always be thrashing, harvesting. There is bread to bake, loaves to be shared.

Truth is a sun often obscured behind clouds of delusion, false idea. For humankind can, in its fear and confusion, manufacture great storms. Still, Truth is a sun. Always search for its evidence: illumination of a leaf, a face, a compassionate heart; and the growing that happens with all living things when touched by Truth.

And you... you are a living, breathing desire. A spirit come from Spirit, who, like a kangaroo joey, just wants to go back inside the place of its beginning. By being fully present and alive in this world, you too may find such peace and contentment. You have a homeland that is Spirit. Always be returning home.

Mohandas K. Gandhi was known to be shy when he was young. Until he was personally lashed by the whips of racism and injustice. These wounds gave him fierce reason, cause, determination, and voice. He was now alive on Purpose.

If you find yourself languishing inside the slog of a humdrum existence, go on an expedition. Search for something in this life that sets your soul on fire. Once you find it—and it is always there if we do not deny it—let it penetrate you deeply... until you can taste your own blood of passion, and know that you are alive on Purpose. The vitality you experience will color your life in a whole new palette of brilliance and meaning. You will be a living work of art, inspiring other living works of art, who want only to be on fire, like the way you burn.

Night is good about staying around until day comes. This allows night to fulfill itself. For us, life's moments are each a bowl of ice cream. We can be like night, and lick the bowl of one moment while we are still in that moment, rather than being distracted by what comes next. What we leave behind as we move through moments becomes the sediment of our suffering. A sense of hollowness becomes pervasive. We never really were present in what we once had, and so we have a hard time bringing fullness and wholeness to what we now have.

There is a reason that night can feel so peaceful and still. Night licks the bowl of its own *nightness*. It does not dream of day, harbor envy of day, or covet what day has. Night licks the bowl of what it is and has. We can become peaceful and still like night, if we learn to lick the bowl of our own moments.

Enjoy your Divine desserts.

Something in the soul wants to be fed its own truth, not the opinions of others. And yet we crave that the world agree with our words and actions. And so we go this way, betraying our soul, starving it from the food of truth, the only food on which soul may thrive.

Graciously, each moment, life offers us another chance to feed our soul. Nutritional choices are not only for the body. They are foremost for the soul. Nutrition that turns away from obeying worldly opinion and turns toward sifting that opinion for truth. A gold prospector will spend months in a cold stream, sifting for golden flakes. Be a prospector. Spend your whole life in the desert of worldly opinions, sifting its sand for grains of truth. This way, you can reliably feed your deepest appetite, which is of the soul.

What the desert does with sand grains, let life do with your heart. Be forever sifted. Allow your contours to change according to the moods of Grace, so that what is rigid in you begins to move as ocean waves. Have your dunes of essence drift over objects and fill in crevasses, until your growth and transformation create a stunning new landmark of natural beauty.

Let your grains pick up in the wind and carry, to become the beginning of something again. And permit your grains to press intimately against one another, until a song lets out that calms us in its purity.

Love happens in the desert between grains. Be *that* Lovemaking in your heart.

Bees work faithfully, with no trace of doubt, to produce the pure, sweet honey we so enjoy. They are completely immersed in their purpose, oblivious to the world.

Friend, please do what you can to remove your mental robe of doubt as you endeavor. Plunge completely into your purpose. Be oblivious to how you are being judged and spoken about, for such buzzing has nothing to do with why you are here. Inside of your purpose, you are an ocean. Oceans do not regard seagull chatter. Being an ocean is too mighty a state of being to focus on anything else.

Keep burning those robes of doubt. See yourself become pure honey for the world.

Bury your worries. Let wild dogs dig them up. Dogs turn human worries into bones to play with. Instead of worrying, excavate your courage. Feast on passion and leave the crumbs behind for the passionless. The whole world is looking for a Lover like you, one who keeps throwing off the covers, feverish for the Truth.

If you don't stop singing, Beauty won't stop arriving. Cue your tongue and pronounce words of Peace. Watch them become seeds of transformation.

Life is a symphony. Don't be one of its musicians frantically turning the sheet music pages while you fumble with your instrument. Be the virtuoso who plays by heart, free and full of the brightest notes.

Some souls *have a faraway look*. They seem to be in another place all the time. Maybe they are at the well, drawing spirit water.

There is a trick to living in this world beautifully. It has to do with our citizenship in another world. Something pure and so very present washes through our mundane reality, making the mundane sacred. Koi fish swim in the ponds we make, but maybe they also swim at the same time in more mystic waters. Who among us can live like this, feet planted on the shore, and spirit swimming in the shoreless ocean? If you find those who can be present in the present, while also being present in the Present (the gift of Sacredness), join them. While others thirst, they are always at the well, drawing spirit water.

We were in Love even before we came into this world. Once here, our Love recognized its Cause, and the sweet weeping started again.

We are old Lovers. So old that our blood and bones have turned into an endless, wild yearning. Because of this duration, anything that is not Love causes us to suffer. Outside of Love, we are like a miserable retiree who has lost his identity, pacing and mumbling aimlessly. Creation has a memory. If we could measure it, we would see:

That's how long we have been in Love.

What swims upstream against the current can often provide our greatest soul reward. Grizzly bears teach us this lesson well. They crouch in the pristine river waters, allowing spawning salmon to fight the current and jump right into their mouths.

Fishing for what is common is easy. All we have to do is go with the common current, the popular trend. Though if we want the prize catch that will sustain us enduringly, sometimes we only need to be willing to open ourselves to the spirit food that runs in a rare direction. After all, like us, it is also headed home.

A pious boy learned quickly from his parents to cast venom at neighbors who did not conform to the religious norms of the community. One day, while the boy was busy scolding others, a woman who lived in the woods suddenly emerged. Her stare silenced and froze the boy. Her words penetrated even deeper:

"Do not spend your precious life judging the holiness of others. For surely, even after a lifetime devoted entirely to faith, you will not have perfected your own holiness. Instead, be consumed with purifying your soul, and let that be the way you touch the holiness of others."

True and lasting Spiritual fertility arises not from coercion. It is a harvest owed to the finer weather of a purifying life, and to those who behold that purity. Like the way moss and mist meet in the wilderness...

and become a forest.

If you are so fortunate as to live your life in the company of a pristine waterfall pouring the clearest water, may you be filled with gratitude. Gratitude being not just thankfulness, but also recognition of the source of the blessing. And a soulful awareness that but for Grace, you would not have your waterfall.

May we, every soul, be today so grateful. For in the innumerable ways of Grace, we are each living our lives in the company of a pristine waterfall.

Look all around you.

Grace is pouring.

We tend to spend so much time and energy intellectualizing over food for our soul instead of eating it. Arguing theologies instead of experiencing *Theos*. Competing over ideas instead of bathing in Truth. Who let the canary into this cave of confusion? It is singing something desperate about how our air is filled with toxic human noise. Yet Hope comes with this quandary:

Canary sees a way out, an opening up above that is filled with light. Because it is a bird, it goes for the opening. Why don't we go for it, too? Of course, to fit through the opening, we would have to strip naked of our identities and ego attachments. Only when we are *quietude* and *humility* do we acquire the shape that fits through the door of Peace. Only when we weave a garment of light with the thread and needle of the mind, are we kindred enough to light that it will let us join the sweetest union.

Admit your need to be warm. Those who on a cold wilderness night sit away from the fire, spend the night in unnecessary tenseness. Say out loud, *I need those flames*, then move closer to the fire and join the unraveling of souls. Embrace your addiction to affection. Don't pretend that for you, kindness is a take-it-or-leave-it proposition. Take it. Keep taking it, until you are soaked with it, and kindness becomes the warmth you seep out as you breathe. Like a child just home from building snow castles, now dripping melted joy all through the house. We need evidence that you have been drinking kindness. Show us *that* side of you. Then prepare to have the kind ones show up to drink what you have on tap.

Offer the world what you want from the world.

Join the fire and sleep warmly tonight.

Grapes are not just hanging out on those winery vines. They are recruiting sweetness to come inside their skin. They have no idea that someone will take their sweetness and ferment it into something else. And that one day they will be valued for a quality that only their original sweetness could produce.

Recruit sweetness into your being in every moment. For, once you have sweetness, you are a promising vintage transforming inside a barrel of life circumstance. Your journey will make your sweetness a new quality, destined to be swallowed by someone thirsty for the exclusive soul elixir you have become.

First though... start with sweetness.

Divine Life is throwing a banquet. We refuse to enter the banquet hall. Divine Life looks out at us, compassionately, saying: *Stop debating food. Come and eat it. Stop analyzing drink. Come and drink it. No more planning to be at Peace. Come be at it.*

Mind is procrastination's greatest playground. Do not abuse your ability to think by lingering on the mental playground when it is time for dinner. Come be fed and leave your ideas on the grass for birds to peck at. Even they won't eat them. They know that to be full, you have to swallow something real.

A waterfall appears to flow in a pattern, over and over. Yet a presence lives inside waterfalls. And were we to ask that presence, "How many times does a waterfall repeat itself?" Presence would answer, "A waterfall does not repeat itself."

"Ever?"

"Not ever."

Some parts of our lives seem to repeat over and over, to the point of painful monotony and malaise. Though if we look deeply enough, with eyes of a child on a treasure quest, we might encounter a presence that entices us: *I'm glad you are finally here. You're about to experience something you've never seen before.*

When our spirit sags, often it is not because of the apparent repetition of waves in our life, but because we have not plunged our face down deep enough into the blessing water.

Forget the scuba gear. Be a diver.

If just one word inside of one sentence, inside of one paragraph, inside of one book, blessed your life... would that book be worth reading?

If just one moment inside of one day blessed your life, would that day be worth living?

And if just one kindness from you inside of this entire world blessed someone's life, would your kindness be worth giving?

We all stare at the ocean, awed and in wonder, and yet we think little of any single drop from that great water. Maybe this is also how we sometimes view our own life: looking for the spectacular cumulative abundance to give our appreciation and value, while missing the Divine abundance inside of the modest and minute.

If you dream of blessing the whole world, then your blessing must be worthy enough for just one person. If joy is worth having, it is worth having for one second. And then another. Let those seconds mate, multiply, and become an estuary of joy. A joyful life.

When did the soul become relegated as an outhouse, while the body is occupied as the main house? Inside of what are we truly living? Sacredness is the best interior designer. It might recommend that we live inside the soul… with mind, heart, and body all residing together there too. What is designed to be whole doesn't do well with its parts scattered. A puzzle is only puzzling when it isn't complete.

Let's live inside the soul. Truly be residential there. Become intimate with its details and nature. And social opinion? Let that stay in the guesthouse. If it gets too rambunctious there, well… there is always the outhouse.

For those who want to be all the way alive, let us live inside the soul.

Inside of ceremonial caves in New Mexico, the ancient Pueblo people left their mark. There, the blackness on the caves' kiva walls is evidence that someone saw the light.

Burn inside. Cover your interior with coal and ash. Have something to clear away so that you can *feel* the phenomenon of discarding what you were. New life makes a garden from burned domains. Fire makes a bargain with Truth: *Give me your old stuff, and I'll give you more of you.* Only bartering like this cracks the code for giving birth.

When forest wants to renew itself, it burns. Burn inside. Disturb the dust and give the dancer that is your soul some original music to move to once again.

Perhaps the best use of Belief is when we allow it to be a midwife, continuously ushering us through the birth canal of enlightenment out into the world of Truth, where all things are made new. Instead, the human condition is that we are so very tempted to use Belief as a fortress, aborting any further soul growth, posing a hard, high wall against any *outside* influence. There, we spend our days, thinking that we are being faithful, when in reality we are being imprisoned for life.

Belief as a midwife only shows up when we put our ego down and realize that we will always be journeying through the birth canal of Truth. *Be humble*. This midwife accepts only humility for payment. Relax your anxieties about *knowing*. And through your *not knowing*, let Midwife's Loving hands massage you into the Light.

Grateful. Wind filling our lungs like sky filling Creation. Grateful. Lives of Loved ones ripening in the orchard that populates our heart. Grateful. Seam in time that lets sweet memories dance with present blossoms, to future's astounding music. Grateful.

The breath of Holy Fragrance inside of all things that makes this world ever so Glorious. Grateful. Pain sacrificing itself so that we have ground to grow from. Grateful. Compassion turning humankind like planet Earth in its gentle palms, spinning us in orbit around the sun of Love. So that we may fall into the splendor of that burning Light. Grateful.

Food in the belly. Drink on the tongue. The desire in us to feed the hungry their daily bread. Grateful. Praise songs called Crying and Laughter. Worship called *Falling in Love*. Grateful. Health like a jewel birthed from a mountainside. Peace like seabirds drafting spring air. And the stillness that lets us notice this gift of being alive. Grateful.

Grace as a sermon in the hum of our humble existence, a warm weather system moving across our valley of days. And Love, the prime calling that brings us together, helplessly bound.

Grateful. Grateful. Grateful.

Peace is a tangible consequence of paying less attention to our own personality and more attention to the personality of Grace. Ruminating less on how we are affected by life and more on how life is affected by us. Forgetting our fickle personal identity and remembering who we are *collectively, soulfully*. Putting down the judgment gavel and picking up the scent of humility. Letting our selfhood leak out and filling instead with Sacredness. Learning to become a tracker of Purity while others keep taking desecration vows.

Peace is a consequence. Be the cause.

We are often consumed with the sand pouring back and forth through the hourglass of our thoughts and emotions. Shatter the hourglass and let your sand blow away. Become consumed with the Wind. Life is a great breeze with the power to purify us from our mental anguish and illusion. It keeps moving, unconditionally. Make your offering. Toss up your pensiveness and hurt into the high breeze of being. Let your angst be carried away as you get carried away with peace.

The way we feel inside is the imperfect echo of a conversation Eternity has within and all around us. Our lives are the tuning fork. Creation is the eager ear. Hopefully, you will grow quiet inside, so that Silence can speak *your* truth. Then may a song arise in you that is wordless. For, when saying becomes being, being is finally said. And when Soul at last says itself, all saying is done.

Come, listen to Silence whisper across the red earth of Creation.

Come closer...

Now we feel the great vacuous gushing of an immense tide going out, and the enormity of what happens when the Ocean reclaims its preciousness. The innumerable distractions of this life cannot keep us from sensing that a very particular soul was with us in our time, one perhaps more intimately acquainted than usual with the tender breath of Grace. And now that soul has changed to the purity of Light. Therefore, is this world not brighter? For even as we in our humanness perceive a loss, in our deeper spiritual sensitivity we grasp a genuine gain. The reservoir of human soulfulness, from which each of us so dearly drinks, has been replenished, filled with the Amandla of Mandela. What was bound by form inside of HE, is free now to be itself entirely, inside of WE. Madiba has joined the Light.

*In honor of Nelson Mandela.

Every soul is a perfume shop to the world. Just because large crowds might enter a particular shop does not mean the proprietor offers quality perfume. Hordes will flock to sourness and bitterness, just as they will come for sweetness and goodness. It all depends on the flock.

The way to tell that someone is offering pure fragrances blended with essential oils like Love and Grace is to pay deep attention to how you feel when you approach the shop. Even before you open the door, your own soul will sing or squawk at the fragrance emanating from inside. For soul essence is like the corona of the sun. It reaches far and penetrates us with its nature.

As for your own fragrance vocation, let us hope that the essences you blend cause what is beautiful inside every soul to smile and beg for the recipe to your perfume.

Some people find that in the early morning they are the clearest spiritual vessel they can be. Early... before others (and they) encroach on the purity they have been swimming in through the night. Before the mist of Sacredness dissipates from their being, evacuated by breezes of thought pollution and social toxicity. If you are one of those who is wide open and infiltrated by Spirit when first awake, this may be a good time of day for you to harvest your spiritual bounty.

Whenever in the day your vessel is most filled with Spirit and wide awake, let this be your harvest time. Do not linger. Gather the inspiration and clarity that speaks to you. Treat it as your most precious harvest, the one your Loved ones and all living things will survive on through the many winters of the soul. Harvest in the ways most natural to you. And make sure you eat, drink, share, preserve, and exercise what you have gathered. Why be a vessel, if what is poured in is never poured back out?

Be a gracious pantry, open for plundering by all who are in soulful need.

As sun goes down into its well of night, moon rises from its mystic burrows. As moon moves against our soul to shed its skin and become something new, the ancestors revive deep inside us. They have seen it all before. And so they beseech us:

Play some good music with your soul. New music, old music, we don't care. Just make your soul music true. Give us something we can dance to.

We are all on our bellies paddling across the emotional lake of our lives. There is always the question of what separates the Peace-filled from the Peace-less on this journey.

Silence cups its mouth and speaks this Truth:

All souls paddle their emotional lake. Most hold their breath while paddling.

A few souls breathe.

Somewhere between breaths of the soul, the true urgencies of your life build a signal fire, wave, and wait for you to spot their encampment. The next time you breathe, breathe with your soul. Let the scent of need-fire reach you. Inhale its singular aroma, then look in that direction for your Sacred urgencies. They will be waving to you, shouting out:

Don't look over there! We are over here. We won't go anywhere. Just, please, come get us.

Once you learn to spot your need-fires from a distance, and from up close, the way a ladybug sees a leaf, you will be so close to the search-and-rescue qualification that living beautifully requires. Most likely, you already have the skills. If so, all that may be left is a burning desire to bring your Divine and wandering needs back home. To the soul.

Ask a hummingbird: *What is it to be new?* Hummingbird might say: *The joy between beats of my wings.*

Plant life might offer: *The way sunlight touches my existence and reminds me that I am alive.*

If in every moment, all things are truly new, something is always being born into this world that has a presence. That presence has a force. Like the way your heart leaps at Hope peering in its window this morning, promising a new day if only your heart would leave its drudgery of chores and come outside and play.

Dreams are clouds showing us what we can move like if we let go of solid things and encamp in the sky of being free. A rainbow jumps from a bush up high into the air and arcs down again, onto another earthly place. It feels new. A little girl wakes and remembers she will be going to the park today. She feels new. When your soul remembers where it was going before this world, it turns in that direction. In that moment, you feel new.

What is it to be new? You, in the way you part open your soul today like a fruit to be eaten by Holiness... you might say:

The Joy between beats of my heart.

Blush like this. Like morning grass. A mountain at sunset. A hawk vibrating to sky's braille of breeze. *Feel* your life, in every moment. Fall into a living dream. Stay there as long as you can. When you find yourself feeling authoritative, you have fallen out of the dream. Fall back in. Feel your life, and you will realize it is not your life. It is the life of every thing.

She is at the open window of an old restored barn house, looking out at the gifts this day has brought her. A field lined with jasmine waves to her with its perfume. Tall grass moves its hips in the wind. Taller trees perform their sentry in stillness. Sky is punctuated with modest clouds. Hawks, ravens, and a rainbow all feel their way in the blue openness.

She remembers once sitting in a tree, wondering how long it had been growing and whether its branch could hold her weight. Now she looks out a window at life pulsing quietly, endlessly. She thinks of the branches of her life, and how, in the end, they each have borne her weight.

Her eyes are on a sparrow. Its small body perches on a bush. With a rhythm of its own, it sings. Its small body is light on the bush, its song even lighter in the air.

She looks out a window, seeing the ways of living displayed for her by nature's vast and wondrous array. She knows she is one of them. *A living thing.*

Sometimes letters, syllables, words, and their various forms of gathering become a chaos in our mind rather than a sacred ceremony. When this is true, Truth cannot breathe. It suffocates while we stumble through the piles, thinking that we are exercising something useful internally.

Truth is like a dog finally let out its kennel onto an open plain of space. It needs to breathe the night air freely. To run to the limits of its endurance. It needs to *feel* itself. Unbridled and unbound.

When our language becomes a cage for Truth, Silence picks the lock. In that space of emptiness, facing freedom, Truth knows what to do. Give your mind emptiness. Behold what Truth gives back to you.

If religion is your path toward Holiness, use that road to travel into the Divinity of Love's village. There, you will be favored with great pots of stew and barrels of drink, all of a nature that burns away your memory of what in this world you are supposed to Love or hate, be drawn to or fear. You will be an amnesiac Lover who does not discriminate.

If you follow scripture, follow it into Love's Divine village and say goodbye to all who choose to stay in the world of conflict and closure. In your new community, you will be ransacked daily by bandits who strip off all of your identity clothes. Once you forget your ideas of yourself, your soul will fill with Light, and you will become a fountain in the village square, pouring out the clearest soul water faithfully.

Whatever is your way to Sacredness, make sure to find your way to Love's enclosure. Which is an Infinite Opening, and the singular point of every path.

Not every bud survives to blossom. And yet, plants still find it worth the effort to keep pushing out more buds.

Our kind tends to grow quickly discouraged when our pursuits don't become perfectly fruitful. We take one instance of an unfulfilled budding as a reason for doubt and giving up. Plants and animals must feel we are odd in this way.

If it is in you to write a book, forgive a trespass, bless your body with health and nutrition, make a new friend, let go of an old habit, learn a new and brighter way of thinking... if it is truly in you to blossom in a way you have not before, then be like all other living things: Continue forward with the impulses for which you were made. Do away with counting the buds that don't make it. Instead, court, cradle, and nurture your impulse to bud. Don't do the math on your buds' survival rate. Just turn over your life to your soul yearnings. And one day, you may find that even your buds are for someone else the very blossom they needed to behold.

We have been given Holy words and Holy ways so that we may be Holy. Not so that we may burn holes of scorn and judgment in our kindred kind. We are peculiar. We often take what is Sacred and use it egoistically to desecrate the Sacredness in others. Maybe this is why your heart sings for a Divine Companionship among the human circle, yet so often receives back only wounded wailing from the masses who are longing, too. Keep singing. Let your notes build into a crescendo of brokenness and surrender. Despair itself is a form of praise, a way for the soul to say: *I see how Great this life can be. I want to be engulfed in THAT Fire and made into a new thing in every day.*

Let us abandon the easy temptation to wrap ourselves in Holy customs and then judge those who still run naked through the streets. Holiness can be tricky. Just when you believe you've found your Holy tribe, suffocating in their layers of heavy Holy-custom clothing, you begin to feel the longing to go running naked, too.

When we enter the soulful sauna of Holy Transformation, we have two choices: We can step inside fully clothed, or we can leave all our clothing at the door. Either way, the Sauna wants our sweat. Not our judgment of humankind.

Say these words inside:

This morning is calm against my soul. Grace is a wondrous vibration running through my chords, dissolving my gatherings of nerve. I am a harp string. Such Hands are playing. Sunlight is the music that emerges. To be touched by Love is a miracle. To gather this Love and touch back is the Purpose. Can I feel the rising? Even as sky's blue deepens, something is lifting into that infinity. Something from here, deep in earth, deeper yet inside of me. The quiet of this moment is enough. Grace speaks for all of us.

Are you seeking caves to hoard your stash? Or are you seeking souls to pour your Love into endlessly? We are either protecting the status quo and our supposed comforts or we are tearing down the house of soul oppression. In a way, life is this simple. We exist either as revolutionary or stationary. Revolutionary does the writing. Stationary (stationery) gets written on.

Authentic Holy Love is a revolutionary fire. It wants only to incinerate all false walls and prisons, fake power and status. It wants to burn down the castles of human fear and ego, and let the masses back inside their Sacred Home.

The deep way you yearn, and what you yearn for, are caused by the same force within us. We believe we want Peace. Peace, though, is an outcome. First, we must find the courage to be revolutionary, to *be* Love. Once Love does what it does, and decimates the castle walls, Peace is the wind that comes blowing so sweetly into our courtyard. Today, make a new world inside your soul. Have faith. Peace has surrounded your castle and is waiting to invade your royal gardens.

In the Koi pond of life, there are those who swim nervously near the surface, waiting for someone to feed them. And then there are those who swim relaxed and Peaceful in the depths. They figure that since they are Koi, and this world is a Koi pond, they are already in the unconditional Presence of what truly feeds them. All they have to do is *be a Koi*.

We are living in the very Divine element for which we were created, dear friend. Know this and be fed.

A *king compulsively stashed* enormous piles of treasure inside a cave. At a fateful point, after hoarding another load, he realized he had sealed himself inside the cave. Though the king was a small man, he had no room to move about this cluttered space. In short time he grew fearful, then lonely, claustrophobic, atrophied, and mad, in that order. He died impoverished, buried beneath the greatest amassed wealth of jeweled treasure this world has ever known.

On the other side of the mountain, at the opposite mouth of the same cave, a devoted student of spirit was busy stashing his own kind of jewels inside his life space: *Love, light, laughter, and Peace*. He was just as consumed with gathering as was the tragic king. At some point, the student's cave was filled with these invisible treasures. The richness exerted a gravity that would not let him leave. Although he was a large man, the cave's abundant spaciousness was so great that he had plenty of room to move amongst his treasure. In no time at all, the apprentice grew awake, alive, and mad with ecstasy, in that order. At last, he died richer than the realm of dreams, drowned in the greatest amassment of material poverty this world has ever known.

Oh yes... and while alive he took a Lover. Their offspring are the waters that run free and sparkling clear in mountain streams.

Your precious mind is like a flock of sheep, and you, my friend, are the shepherd. Your flock of thoughts is born to wander and graze. Without guidance, it may often find its way into harmful places and routines. Without your shepherding, the flock will not choose the premium grass to graze, nor will it find its drinking water. It will not rest when it needs to, for it is energetic by nature and contagiously anxious. In the end, it will not reproduce fruitfully, with healthy offspring.

Gather your shepherd staff and renew your practice. It is time to lead your flock to the lush grass of healthy thoughts, and the pure drinking water of soulful communion. Condition your flock to rest and be still regularly, so that it may be revitalized each day. Nurture your flock, so that it may reproduce healthy offspring: positive thoughts that in turn birth yet other wholesome inner conversations.

Do not allow your flock to be like so many other flocks, scattered and bleating neurotically. You are the shepherd. Lead your mind to prime pasture and water, then take it faithfully back Home. Watch your flock grow calm and efficient, its bleating as soft and tender as a lamb.

Even dawn does not know what to do with your Glory. So it spreads your Light across the sky and over all that textures this earth. Look into your nature with spiritual eyes. See how Creation's entire gallery is woven into your being. Your matter is kindred to all matter. Your bones descend from the trees and stones of this world. Your emotions have many relatives flowing as rivers and streams. Your thoughts are sparks in a human conversation that is on fire with Consciousness. And the sun is sibling to your radiant heart.

The reason you ache and awe before the beauty of nature is because nature *is* your nature. You gaze at your origin, and, like a fawn spotting its mother, you recognize the awesome epiphany that is Grace. The only place you care to be.

She sang this song all through her days, to tune her heart to Glory, to harmonize her soul with Grace:

Lo, I have heard the angels sing in their ethereal realm. Of this I need no proof, for my soul is a cathedral the angels do attend, and my every pew and pillar is soaked and weeping praise.

We may know the legacy of a river eons after its lifetime, by its carving of the earth, its historical shaping of terrain. Like the way we become acquainted with the intimate touch of a clay worker's hands by our beholding of her pottery.

Our own lifetime is a river, too. Ultimately, our legacy will be known by the way we shape this collective human soul, and the fine residue we leave behind. The grains and essence of our Love and Compassion.

Who we are now will not one day be sitting on a shelf like precious pottery. *Who we are now* will be alive and radiant in the shape and substance of who this humanity will come to be. You, friend, are creating the world. May your soul-hands work beautifully.

She spreads out a soft blanket on the belly of the tall grass in a bright, open field. Wistfully, she lays all afternoon, staring at cloud messages in the rich blue sky, daydreaming about her life. Her heart reminds her that it desires to be Loved. Longing sparks in her. Yearning for intimacy, caring, companionship.

Just then, a deer appears from the woods and, magically, approaches her. Its soulful eyes seem to be communicating affection. The deer comes so close, she feels she could touch it if she reaches out. The deer bows its head, nudges the grass, seems playful, beckoning. Her heart dissolves in an awe of warmth and joy. She realizes: *Love is always with her*. She grows content. The field becomes her paradise, her fulfillment. She lets go of the definitions of Love she has been taught. She finds the truth of Love. No longer desperate, fearful, in despair, she becomes an open vessel. Love, in its essential forms, comes rushing in.

Friend, Love is always attracted to you. It always wishes only to be with you. Look with new eyes upon the way life's spirit, which is Love, gravitates toward your being. Especially as your being... relaxes and radiates Love.

The direction of Joy is not inward, it is outward. The personality of Love is not closed, it is open. The mood of Compassion is not cold, it is warm. To surrender is not weak, it is strong. To bow in honor is not to shrink, it is to enlarge. What we want most is inside us, not apart from us. And the nature of your own life is not improbable, it is forever possible.

Someone taught us an upside-down lesson in a backward classroom. And so, being obedient students, we suffer. It is time not for obedience, but for freedom of the soul and the clarity it brings. We have been given sacred eyes to see sacred things. You have to *see* a vision before you can *be* a vision. Watch out. You just looked inside your sacredness. *Now you've been seen.*

This life has a beautiful, joyful side. In every single moment, it wants your attention. It has something for you. If you can, dear soul, turn in that direction. Turn repeatedly, devotedly. You will become springtime. And your worries will become wildflowers in the rising radiance of an awesome sun.

Human suffering makes a cave of days. We on earth are looking for a volunteer to light the torch and show the way. You don't have to be brave. Just weary of this stumbling blindness.

Here, hold the Sacred fire. Now... just start walking forward. Just by holding the Light, you share the Light, and illuminate our human way. Soon, the cave opens out into fresh air. Surrenders its darkness. Soon, bright lagoon. When it comes to happiness, you have your choices. You are not helpless on this path to Hope. You are where Hope begins.

If you are not digging daily deep into the soil, asking, *Why am I here*, then perhaps you are not fully here. Nothing releases us into the sweet arms of Peace and Presence like an epiphany of Purpose. Wonderfully, when we dig deeply enough, we each arrive at the very same groundwater. The sanctifying ointment that is the very breath of Creation: *The spirit of Love*. Not sappy confection. Absolute, demanding Sacredness. The profound reverberation that composes all things.

Be composed today. Dig deeper. You are waiting for *you* beneath the soil.

Every moment has its sunrise, sun peak, and sunset. Its expression of Sacred Will. When we learn to move in this supernatural harmony and rhythm, we are getting the most out of life. We are preciously squeezing our moments. Fresh juice is produced. When we learn to make deep use of these seeds planted in us, we become a forceful garden. Fruitful. Fulfilled.

Our life is not for our sake, but for the world's. The more efficient we are in harvesting what is planted in our moments, the more we have to share. The more plentiful our harvest, the more bountiful the meal of the masses. And in return, the more abundant our inner spring of Grace.

You are here, in this world, because you have been made to give. To open, part, and pour. To share, merge, and wed. To pollinate and flower. To increase the Light in all things. Keep learning your own way of moving inside the sunrise, sun peak, and sunset of your moments. This is how you grow your Peace.

Some touch weeds, and the weeds become roses. Some touch roses, and the roses become weeds.

Some speak, and the whole world glistens with the sweetest dew. Some open their mouths, and flocks of rabid bats come flying out.

Some walk through the world leaving crumbs that become loaves in the hearts and souls of those who find that trail. Some leave only seeds of hurt and pathology in their wake.

We need you to be a rose maker. A Light speaker. A walker who brings fresh bread. You need this, too. That is why you keep leaping toward beauty, like a living thing toward the promissory Sun.

We cherish those moments when we feel so happy, so alive. We wish we could keep that feeling going. Instead, we peak, then slide. Glow, then dim. Some souls seem to have tamed the rollercoaster. They appear to remain in a joyful place, consistently.

If you are not one of those, take comfort. For this life offers us its secrets every day. Our *belief* in the possibility of unconditional joy may be a key factor. For if we believe joy is possible, we will strive persistently to awaken it.

One way to work on our belief in joy is to work on our disbelief in joy; a disbelief rooted in fear and misunderstanding of reality. Assess the myths you tell yourself. Bring them out into the light. One by one, release them. Keep releasing them every time they come up. Learn to recognize when they come up. Be in tune, in touch with your false stories. Gradually, as your *joy-disbelief* fades, your *joy-belief* flourishes. And with belief, all things are possible. Even joy.

How often is kindness a calculus you run through your system, considering whether it is worth the risk? Your greater risk is in not daring to be kind. Your life is a great, wide valley. Spores grow in your ground. You put them there. Some of the spores are healthful for you: *warmth, compassion, reverence*. Other spores are poison: *coldness, condescension, spite*. Whatever you have interred in your earth, spores will be spores. They are made to lift into the air, break open, and enter you. Once they are in your lungs, your bloodstream, your bones, those spores do with you what they were made to do: Multiply.

Culture is a parent, and this culture raised us to be more concerned with the risks of kindness than with the risks of not being kind. Go back to school. Become a new kind of risk assessor. Shine a light on what the soul loses when it does not fulfill its Loving nature. Go forth and spread your ministry of kindness. Smile. Let Love show through your gifted eyes. Loosen your tight constitution and be willing to pour a warm cup of humanity for all that crosses your path. If you do this, it is promised: *Warmth will pour Itself back into you.*

To a dog, or a squirrel, you may seem like a tidal wave, or a mountain blotting out the sun. Perspective is everything. You may feel that your sullenness is a small thing, and yet to a child in your vicinity, it is a heavy blanket pulled over the sky. You may feel that your warm, Loving energy is not noticed by anyone, much less the world. Yet, to a youth who has always been treated coldly, you have just brought global warming to her entire soul.

You are not only what you think you are. You are also what life around you, and even distant from you, experiences you as. Let this humble you, empower you, leave you mindful, careful, and tuned in as you choose to speak, act, think, and feel. You are a force to be reckoned with. Be joyfully sensitive as you reckon with yourself. Don't just leave footprints in the sand. Leave a softer sand.

Morning. Your soul still aloft with angels. Bring that company down here to earth. Show them around the spaces of your life. Introduce your dusty corners to the brilliance of Being. You know the way. Calm your inner existence.

Be like dawn: Peel back your darker layers. Let sun rise in the way you live this day. Loosen the bindings around your heart. Give back to what gives you life. To what life gives you. Share some warm feelings with cold souls. They suffer. You can lift their heavy cloudbank. As they brighten, they can take your own dusk away.

Your relationship with your life is like a child at the park. If it rains, you can sit under some sort of cover and sulk. Or you can run, laughing wildly, to a sliding board and make it an awesome waterslide.

What vines do with each other in the jungle, do that with your positive thinking. Let the bright coiling be so thick and overgrown, nothing else can get through. Peace is a matter of physics. When a space is filled with one thing, it cannot be filled with another. Life has its troubles. You have your mentality. Don't be a rain barrel for whatever toxin drops from the sky. Be filled with Light, like an incandescent lantern. You don't see any shadows creeping inside that fire.

People won't be as likely to tempt you with their ill spirit if your vessel spills over with Grace. Swim with dolphins in your mind. They will show you where the water is shark-free and melts like sugar against your emotion. Lift your spirit. It is not a bottom feeder. It wants to be a kite.

If you weren't such a tender-hearted soul, you could not *FEEL* this profound life. *Of course* you hurt. You are a raindrop held against the needle of life's harshness. But because you are a raindrop, you also magnify life's sunlight throughout your soul. Happiness uses you to become what it is. Use your sensitivity to become what you are:

Love.

A single cave. We humans are a tribe inhabiting a single cave, each of us striving to leave our mark on the walls. Some of us strive frantically, others calmly. We are all born hieroglyphic artists, with a need to express our existence. If you feel that your artwork is being crowded out by that of others, or that you don't have elbow room to do your work, or if you just feel the need for fresh air, don't be afraid to leave the cave and step into sunlight.

A cave exists beyond this worldly cave. After all, your inspired expression is nothing other than the soul-dipping we do in the Unseen Ocean. Yes, you want to express your life in this tangible world. Yet, your life originates from the Intangible. Of course you yearn for a larger cave… the cave within. Breathe. Settle. Be still. Remember Peace. Remind yourself: *I am not in an emergency. I am in Life. I am free to live.*

Do this, and your cave may open up into a cavern of bigger, brighter walls, each eager for you to bless them with your living art.

Morning is a clear mountain stream in which we may wash our soul, and begin a new day with the freshness of blue sky after summer rain. Fill your palms with this clarity of an awakened sun. Splash your face and eyes in the coolness. Renew your weariness. Today, you have been given an entirely new circle of life. Discover the silent and shining way it turns for you.

Word of your heart's tenderness has reached the outer limits of the universe. Maybe that is why all that has a soul finds its way to you: So that you can caress its need to be Loved. And it, in turn, can touch your heart with the miracle of gentleness. Pain you feel was already siphoned off beforehand by Compassion. You only experience a sliver of that, an amount you can bear. And the Joy your heart wakes to is only an invitation to a much Greater Joy.

See how you are Loved? A catering service has been hired for your heart. Your exclusive heart. You are being catered to, precisely. Your own tenderness is being served to you, as a delicacy. Let yourself be served.

Your heart whispers the most wonderful things to you. Such as this:

I want the faraway land in your eyes. The orchards that whisper, the casual brooks that speak a language of water and reeds. Take me from this outpost and plant me deep, down where earth hums and warms. Beneath rocks and their resistance. Where you are soft and giving, and decided upon your fertile fate, that is where I want to be.

Don't be afraid of silence.

It's where you find your song.

Don't fear being alone.

Aloneness as a bad thing is a cultural myth, an untruth that causes suffering. In aloneness you can find your greatest togetherness. Your soul and life are both companions whose most reassuring presence is felt when you have arrived all the way to your precious self.

They told us that when we grow up, life is going to be great, because we'll be free to live life as we choose. Funny, it seems as though most of us lived most freely as children, and the more we grew up, the less we chose to truly live. Maybe we shouldn't grow up. Maybe instead we should remember freedom.

Good news. Life brings things together.

Good news. Life takes things apart.

Good news. In every moment, we get to touch and be touched by the good news. If we see this endless cycle of change as a gift of life, tension leaves us, joy has room to enter, and we become for those we encounter a singular embodiment of good news.

If you feel empty inside, spend some time inside of true emptiness. It has a way of filling you up. Yearning and desire can be like cotton candy. We are tempted to fulfill them by consuming their attractiveness. In the end, they are only sugar that inflames and overflows the spaces inside meant for the lightness of our true nature. A nature that is already complete.

Judging others is like fantasizing about mowing your neighbor's lawn, while your own lawn continues to be overgrown with weeds. Judgment throws fuel on the fire of our soul neglect, and casts shade through our interior, where fungus then thrives. A better way to relate is to become so swollen with Love that even your eyes fill with affection. That way, you will no longer be able to see anything to judge.

Crazy thing about Love. The more you share it, the more it is shared with you. The more you dream it, the more it becomes your living dream. The more you remember it, the more you are remembered by it. The more you surrender to it, the more it surrenders to you. The more you look for it in the simplest ways, the more it finds you in your simplicity. And, of course, the more you live for it... the more it lives for you.

If you often feel a binding sensation in your life, like a butterfly yearning to shed its chrysalis, stretch its wings, and take flight... there is a reason. We cannot have our fullest Peace within until we shed our Peace into the world. We are each a galaxy of a million suns, forever straining to release that power. And though we run from it in endless ways, it is our calling. Fulfillment comes through surrender. Those who shine have released their sun to a needful world. For they know the truth. The human soul is a single whisper:

Share your Light.
Share your Light.
Share your Light.

It is likely that you underestimate the potency and value of your personal kindness. Are you like so many others, who say to themselves: *This world is so large and filled with rage and hurtfulness. What is my kindness but a drop of water against a consuming fire?*

If this is you, then you have been deceived. The human soul is so vulnerable and in need. Even the kindness of one may tilt the human garden away from ruin and toward vitality. So much desire and want permeates this world. And you possess a power that you gravely underestimate: your kindness, warmth, tenderness, affection.

Even chocolate wants your kiss. Go ahead...

Make it melt.

What is Love but the unrationed tide of your lips of desire against the deep drawn tender shore you seek? What is Love but the rampaging wilderness of your heartbeat, overgrown, un-landscaped, pillaging tidy lawns with its wildflowers, its meadows of moonlight and delinquent red sunrises?

What is Love but the ardent, rampant ache, the redundant yearning, the drunken mist, sideways world, dousing fragrance, obliteration of your composure before the beauty before you, the roused beauty of your dreams, unimaginable architecture and floral breath of the deep sea and naked universe to which you cannot help but to give away all your atoms, all your molecules, all your essence, for just one taste of this mango of life, this papaya of passion, this unrevoked passport to that privately public landscape of river song and romance, of stampeding sublimity, of moaning, mystic, mountainous Union.

Today is a basket you carry for harvesting life. Don't let the sun go down with you holding an empty basket. Fill it... all the way to overflow. Bring home the feast. Bend low. Reach high. Pluck the ripeness from every vine. Unearth the richly soiled treasures. This is not just a movement through the day and its happenings. You are a happening, and this is your day. Fill up your basket.

When it comes to participating in life, don't be the frightened child holding up the wall at the school dance. Be the child who never leaves the dance floor, and who could not care less whether anyone else is dancing. Be like this with the music that is your life.

A rose opens to the presence of sun, and says to us, *Do as I do, only do it to the presence of Love.* Flowers are great teachers. They have no speeches, scripts, or syllabi. They just show us how to be a blossoming thing.

Beauty is a divine gift meant to hush the mind, summon the heart, and surrender the soul. Make sure you open the gift today. Splash it on your skin, an invigorating cologne. Pour it down your throat, a cool, fresh tonic. Wear it as spectacles, coloring everything you see. Make it your soundtrack. Your dance partner. Your inner guru. Beauty is a divine gift. Open your eyes of optimism and wonder. Let yourself be gifted.

On the brighter side of life… Recognize that hate is but one way fear chooses to express itself. When you encounter hate, be assured, you are encountering a soul in the throes of fear and suffering. Find the will and the reason to summon your compassion. In doing so, not only will you douse hate, but you will bless your heart and being with clear, unpolluted skies.

And when you encounter Love, know that you have just crossed paths with a convict escaped to freedom from hate's penitentiary. Celebrate and honor others for such accomplishments, for this world holds many traps. Those who manage to stay free and Loving deserve our applause.

Here's to the freedom in you.

Dawn breathes once more, pulling back its dreamy blanket of mist as if to say:

Rise, sweet souls. A new miracle of life offers itself to you today. Step inside its breast of Light and be new like endless dawns. Trade out your old spirit and, with every chosen breath, be new. Be new in your unrehearsed emotion. Be new in your birthing of unprecedented habit. Let your taste, touch, and smell be new. Renew your life. Replenish your ocean. Let go of acquiring. Acquire letting go. Give your heart this gift. Be new.

In a truly creative life, making a mess is the first step toward making a masterpiece. Your perfectionism is a habit. Mess-making can be one, too. Practice unleashing the free-spirited child artist in you. Mantra this key to freedom:

I can create my life. I give myself permission.

Engrave your day with the calligraphy of Love. Care about the lines and curves that you leave on the canvas, the swirls and flourishes that are your personal art. People are reading and gazing your creativity. They want to *feel* your message. Breathe like a painter deep in the silence. Use your best brushes and lose your appetite. You are a vessel now, in purposeful motion. Imprint us with Love.

Enlist your life in Beauty. Be subscribed. You see, a beautiful life doesn't go around implanting itself in dry, hard ground. You must choose it. Your soul decision sends a wave of energy through the world, unlocking the mystery of peace. Now you have begun the whispering that runs through life, the telling of your choice to bloom. Sky wakes, wind follows, seeds and pollen swim toward you. You open and receive, openness reciprocates. Now you see beauty. Beauty sees you. A Love commences that never ends, a prologue to generations of peace.

Carve your life like a sacred totem pole. Make its features mean something. Good spirit flocks to totems, resides in the wood and grain. The best ones become beacons, signaling the presence of Sacredness and honor. If you want others to treat you this way, carve your life into Sacredness. Thought by thought, memory by memory, breath by breath. These are the building blocks. Your behavior is the scalpel. You are a powerful being. Like any totem, your ancestors live in you.

Peace is not a destination. It is an excavation. Continue removing the dirt. Seasons have left many layers of sediment covering your soul's original peace. The soiling is subtle and gradual, which is why we often don't see our peace burial coming. One day, we look around and realize peace cannot be seen. We go looking out in the world. This is our first mistake. Peace is not a vacation spot, a distant wonder of the world. It is a glory within the soul. Put away your travel guide, my friend, and kneel down in the soil of your truth. You will get dirt under your nails doing this kind of work, and many suns will rise and set. But with patience and faith, and a stillness that brings clear memory, you will begin to see the glint shining up from your sediment. Once you unearth your treasure, keep it clean by using it daily as the *centerpeace* to your life.

Imagine happiness. Now, you are halfway there. Seeing is an act that plants a seed. This seed of seeing becomes a sprout of being. If happiness feels far away, you are suffering from a common illusion. As humans, we deal in identity, which can be as fragile as a dream, and as misleading as a nightmare. See yourself happy. Envision yourself joyful. Keep seeing. Each repetition erases the false identity that says, *I am not a happy thing*. Happiness itself is just a word, an idea, a social breeze. Beyond all these illusory identities is the truth that your soul is a divinely joyful thing. How do we know this? Because the nature of life is joy. Expansive, unconditional, fertile, outward energy. If you are alive, you, dear, are a joyful thing. If you don't feel this way, keep seeing, keep seeding. Soon, you will be.

There is a sun inside every sand grain. Just as there is a fire inside every soul. Pick up a sand grain, and you may not see the sun inside, but it is there. Sun inspires all living things, and a grain is a living thing. You may not recognize the fire in your soul, but it is there. As Love. Love inspires all living things. Without it, you would not remain alive. Your task is to be your own fire keeper. Many of us give more to tending the fires in those we Love, those we serve, than to our own flame. A flame can be a fragile thing. Stay close to yours. It has a personality and speaks many languages. You need to be fluent, so you can respond to your own need. And remember, your greatest need might simply be *to share your fire*.

Your ancestors live inside of you. Their voice causes you to have no peace unless you are being true to you. Quiet them. Give them reason to leave you in peace. You think you are clever, that you can get them to go away by giving them crumbs from your partial peace. But they want the entire bread. They want it fresh, and alive, and steaming. They want your true Peace. This is the way of harmony, of the Diné tradition *Nizhoní, the Beauty Way*. You can be in alignment with the dreams of your ancestors by being in alignment with your instinct, intuition, spirit voice. This ability takes plenty of silence and time walking through the land that is your soul. Create such a life. Give peace to your ancestors. They in turn will grant you peace.

The soul speaks in a language only the soul can hear. It speaks to itself. This is why we must stay home in our own soul. You may often be tempted to go out wandering the streets outside your soul. Maybe to visit or even move into another person's soul. This street life will only bring you pain. Come home. You have no need to feel anxious at home. You aren't missing anything. In truth, you are in the presence of everything. You can only miss something if you are not home. Home is where you are wide open and in touch with all things. Stay home. You will hear the most incredible language. And you will understand its healing words.

Liberate your compassion. Quarantine your disregard. This life, this human life, is for caring. Without that, we are housesitting in an outhouse, with no hope for payment. Move into your true residence: Caring. It is perfect for you. Fresh air through endless windows. Vaulted ceilings that let you kiss the sky. And sweet water pouring through the faucets that ends your every thirst. When you feel like not caring, you are like a child afraid to belong, so you want to scurry out into the streets. Hold yourself back. Freedom is when you choose to open your compassion windows and take off all the locks.

Once, there lived a woman who had an infinite heart. Where suffering flared, she found it. Sat by it. Took its hand. Walked with it. Helped to build it up. She caught many tears in her caring palms. Listened to endless sorrow stories. And always, she granted the suffering their dignity. She had faith and hope, which she shared like bread and water. She admired the lowest as the highest. She put the least first. She forever stood for truth and honor.

Others asked her, "How do you care so much? Don't you ever get burned out? Feel hopeless?"

She answered, "I serve the soul. Burnout and hopelessness are the divine gardens where I gratefully work. I am called by Sacredness to be a torch of compassion. As long as I drink from the endless reservoirs of Grace and Goodness, I have all that I need to serve every soul. I learned long ago that when opened to the infinity of Love, a human heart becomes infinite. I am a soul worker. Which is another title for one whose heart has lost its boundary, and gained Amazing Grace."

Let your next breath be your first moment in the world again. Reignite wonder in your heart. Make all things new. Breathing has this power. Inhale intentionally. Know that you are inhaling life. Feel life enter you, move through your body and being, blessing everything along its way. This breath is your very first saturation in the spirit of life. So is your next breath. When you exhale, release all the false ideas planted in you by the world, and all the emotions generated by those ideas. Exhale your illusions. Lovingly set them free. They don't belong to you. They aren't your property, though they have grown like vines through your identity. Set them free. Each breath, bring home life and take out the trash. Each breath. Be new.

All of our life we search for happiness. Which is like a meadow searching for *meadowness*. Truly, we are the very nature of happiness: *Love, Joy, Wonder, Expansion, Discovery*. We aren't lacking happiness. We just so often bury it under quests for false fulfillment. No more searching. Just being. Watch what rises from your divinely planted ground.

Be like a bee. *Just be*. Then see how much honey you make of your life. Lose yourself in your most passionate things. This is how the soul sings. Saturation in what makes us buzz. Earn your peace by doing nothing at all but deeply being. Deeply being is an art, a craft we polish by returning faithfully to the flower, faithfully to the hive. Back and forth between what fills us and the purposeful filling we do. *To bee or not to bee*, that is the question that sets us free.

Catching Peace is not like catching a cold or catching your breath. It is not a matter of catching, at all. It is a matter of letting go. Some of the most intelligent souls never achieve Peace because they approach it as something to be caught, like prey in a spider's web.

Some of the most uncelebrated souls, however, know deep and lasting Peace, for they realize that Peace is our innate potential, the light inside the web. We need only stop weaving, stop worrying, stop waiting... and simply let the light emerge. Like fresh spring water seeping out from newly exposed soil.

With fishing, we catch and release. With Peace, we release, and therefore we are caught.

In Peace.

In the lighthouse of the soul, an intensity cuts through all the darkness and mist. A persistent radiance of being that serves as a beacon for all vessels lost on the waters of existence. It calls out to us: *Come this way! Safe landing ahead.*

In the lighthouse of the soul is an intensity, pure and persistent.

Keep shining.

What does it mean to be divergent, after all, but to submit to the glory of your own soul rather than to the sum of human fears, that flawed wind leading to fateful cliffs of desolation. What is divergence but the peeling away of remarkability from the trodden path of mediocrity, and the sublime sermon of the spirit thereafter, *languaged* in freedom, alight and verifiably alive. Where two paths emerge from one in a moment of your truth, and one goes toward Commonplace, follow your deepest surge.

Diverge.

We have two choices when presented with Today: Live it as a miracle, or move through it as a monotony. Living miraculously takes practice, but only because we have learned the habit of monotony. *Train for miracles*. As they happen in each and every moment, your heart of wonder will know what to do.

Tears are the pure dance the soul does when it is moved so deeply it cannot help but flood the world into being more soulful. Be not ashamed or hesitant with your tears. A drought is happening all around you, a soullessness. You carry rain that can bless the tribe. When the soul dance in you stirs, some mystic music must be at hand, a spiritual enticement. Be a sacred dancer. When your tears come, let them sing and hum, let them drum and praise the sun. Let them flow, a salvation storm to soak the world in soul.

A shepherd left his home in the early morning to bring his flock from the pen up to the mountain meadow to graze. Before he left, he took off his night clothes, and put on his day clothes. He picked up his staff and stepped out into day.

When he and his flock reached the meadow, he gave thanks for the sun, sky, rain, and earth. His flock went about grazing, bleating, and napping. When the sun dropped to one-sun above the horizon, the shepherd led his flock home. It was a good day. No stress. No rushing. Just moving peacefully through moments.

A moral can be found here: When it is time to sleep, sleep. When it is time to wake, wake. Make sure to take off your emotional clothes from the previous moment, and dress properly for the one at hand. Give thanks. For everything. Pick up your staff of faith and fortitude, and lead your flock of heart, mind, and soul through a good day of grazing. Be well fed.

Each day offered to us is like a divine mouth. It wants to taste your sweetness. Return the offering. Pick your best crops of emotionality. Harvest your lushest fruits from the orchard of your journey. Spill your heart like vintage wine for the thirsty. Recall your brightest moments and send out *that* energy to the masses. Don't be a high-priced deli, selling mediocre cuts. Be a delicacy, and charge nothing for the blessing.

In order to be true to yourself, you must know yourself. In order to know yourself, you must know stillness. In order to know stillness, you must remember Peace. In order to remember Peace, you must forget despair. In order to forget despair, you must cleanse from fear. In order to cleanse from fear, you must renew faith. In order to renew faith, you must recognize falsity. In order to recognize falsity, you must be true to yourself. Being true, then, is the practice that sets you free.

A sage taught her student to be like a willow tree. Now, the student knows stillness, even as she dances at the slightest breeze.

Courage is the convergence of will, purpose, and faith. Purpose and faith together are an alchemy that creates your will. Exercise your will and you polish the face of your purpose. Seeing the beautiful face of your purpose renews your faith. Faith is a continual baptism that cleanses your soul of all but purpose. This is how these three rivers birth courage, a fire that resurrects your soul.

Be like the sun.

Live in such a way that life on earth cannot wait for you to rise each morning.

Be *that* kind of Light.

Solar power is nothing compared to soul power. Solar power can energize civilizations. Soul power can energize endless generations and heal humanity back to being human. If you want to invest in the most promising renewable energy, pour yourself into a life of the soul.

Keep Love flowing through your soul. Love is the divine ointment that keeps the soul supple and fluid. Without Love, your soul is a riverbed without water. A sky without air. Life without beauty or Grace. The Love we speak of here is not romantic possession. True Love is a freedom that touches everything with Creation song, granting sunrise to the soul. Be an endless *soulrise*. Make Love.

A *life without compassion* is a night sky empty of moonlight and starlight. It sits heavy and mortal upon the soul, a burden to the world. Flood your heart with a deep, boundless caring. It will raise you up from melancholy into a bright plateau of union. You will feel like your own daylight, and joy's breeze will stay with you faithfully.

Your life is a miraculously abundant life. This is true regardless of circumstance. It's just that we humans are walking through a fruitful orchard, sometimes seeing with the wrong eyes, causing us not to recognize the fruit. It is true, the more you reach for, pluck, and taste the fruit of your life, the better you will be at reaching, plucking, tasting. Yet if you do not see the fruit as fruit, no harvesting skill will help you. Stillness gives us true vision. Slow down. Step away from the carnival. Take a deep breath outside the circus tent. Stay in your spirit and you will see this world for what it is, and Sacredness for what it offers. Be like a child who goes wandering in the forest and ends up with the juice of wild berries all over her smiling face.

Birds flock to trees that have an inner stillness, no matter how much their branches move. Peace flocks to souls with an inner stillness, no matter how much turbulence is in their life. Sometimes we focus too much on calming the waters of our life, and not enough on calming our soul for its journey over the waters. We have more control over our inner life, so investing here with reflection, contemplation, purging, healing, and beautifying yields more benefit. Inner life is the soil from which outer life emerges. Peace has a taste for stillness. Let it flock to you.

A mountain of courage will rise from your fear, if only you would exercise your faith. *More reps. Less weight*. More practice. Less worry about fleeting, grandiose shows of faith. Grain by grain, build your fortress. Courage will rise in you like spring water wakened and alive. Fear will flee, for it is a false fountain flowing inside your forgetting of your truth. Remember, you are a purposeful thing. Purpose made you for this.

Your soul cooks a divine stew. All that remains is for you to serve the feast. Much of our suffering comes from holding onto the goodness in us that is meant for others. Goodness is not ours to possess. It is ours to share. By hoarding it, it sours and loses its divine composition. The perfect stew of seasoning and stock can turn to a sour mush if we are not continuously ladling it out to a world in need. When you feel most hungry in the soul, it may be that a greater hunger is calling for your nutrition. Don't confuse this signal. There is a time for you to eat, and a time for you to serve.

You can find eternity inside of silence. Isn't eternity the essence of what we yearn for? To comprehend and feel the presence of something that will not leave us, not forget us, not leave us grieving? Permanence. We cannot find it in the common world, though it thrives in the unseen mystery weaving our lives. Silence is such a garden. Don't fail to see it. Use your gifted eyes. Sit in this garden and breathe yourself back to your soul. Eternity will appear from the bushes, already formed and blushing. When you find yourself anxious about the temporal nature of things, leave the world of things and join eternity waiting for you Inside of silence.

Nothing is more enormous than the smallest things. Our culture may be the kind that teaches us to look for and see the grandiose. This can cause us to miss the wonders of the smallest grain. Minute particles make this life: cells, molecules, memories, heartbeats, breaths. Everything spectacular is composed of the sublime. If you practice developing vision for essence, essentially you will give birth to seeing. Celebrate sound, soul, surrender, silence. And the circumference of a dew drop on a petal. The true wonders of the world are unassuming. You don't have to travel to them, and no camera can capture the life they make for you. Look more closely. This is how you find Peace.

The way a mountain sits in stillness and ponders. *Inspiration for a peaceful life.* Each day, endless classrooms are available to you, with myriad lessons on the truth of things. Study the sky, wind, trees, butterflies, living things. Observe your relationships with a compassionate eye. Pay attention to the drumbeat of the world, the dance of Creation, and the ceremony of suffering souls. Bow down and analyze healing in an orchid, an aphid, an apple tree. Peer into a crystal, a geode, an obsidian stone. Each tells a story of a journey of time and relation. If you feel you need more learning or awareness, open to ever-present teachers in your life. They have no office hours, for they are always with you.

Pain carves you. You can become a hopeless abyss. Or you can become a grand canyon. The difference is in what you do with pain. First, recognize that it is not *your* pain. It is a current moving through you. Let it come out the other side. Otherwise, that river may crest and breach and flood you. And consider that pain is not a negative or positive thing. It is a potential. Energy waiting for your command. Let the artist in you have a field day. Say these words: *Okay, pain, I am going to use your sharpness to sculpt the most beautiful life I can imagine. Then, I am going to go beyond my imagination. Like the Grand Canyon to the ancient water that made it, I am going to give you away.*

If you are going to burn with Love, don't hold back. Devour every soul, every single living thing. Your Love is an incense that intoxicates the whole world. Never stop burning.

In a world that can continuously erode you, it is necessary that you validate yourself relentlessly. Dress for the weather. If you live in a rainy climate, you learn to dress to stay dry. In the desert, you cover your skin from the burning sun. In paradise, you shed your clothing. And, dear friend, in a world of stress, anxiety, and soullessness, it helps to fill yourself with peace, calm, and soul. Strange voices spill like bats from caves of ignorance, telling you ugly tales of who you are. You know this, so dress for the climate. Move through your day speaking to yourself mantras of your truth. Reassure yourself all day and night. This is not insecurity. It is you learning to be your most priceless masseuse.

Curate your own soul. It is a priceless artifact. This is not a question. What is unsure is whether you preserve your soul the way it deserves. Your ancestors once dreamed you. In their dream, you were a perfect light they caressed in their hands and spilled tears of Love over. And now? Has your soul been scattered in the winds of human disregard? Go looking for it. *In here*. In you. Collect the pottery shards and arrowheads. Remember your ceremonies. Instead of spending life gathering other people's essence and displaying that as your identity, grow your own gallery, filled with your own medicine and stories. And open your doors only to those who know how to enter sacredly.

Be interested only in freedom and the singular path that takes us there: *Love*. All else in this world is a distraction from the truth. The truth of our divine nature and human suffering. Speak words of freedom. Write words of freedom. Dream freedom. Remember freedom. Dare, conceive, create, resolve freedom. Stay on the path. Let no one or nothing cause you to disembark. Get free. Stay free. Free the people.

When we meet someone who feels like a clear, endless sky, we may be tempted to pour all our anxieties into that sky. But this would leave the sky heavy and obstructed. Limited, anxious, impatient. The sky would no longer be what we were so drawn to in the first place. When you meet such a person, behave like a bird. Draft the sky gratefully, and leave it. Leave it clear and free. You will find this creates in you your own endless sky.

Love has never been found as a root of hate, nor hate as a root of Love. The two cannot coexist. Therefore if you flood any space—soul, relationship, striving—with Love, hate cannot live there. Hate is a bacterium that breeds in Love's absence. Love is a miracle that can bloom anywhere. And does. Do the daily inner gardening that fills your soul with beauty and leaves no room for anything but Love.

May your day be painted in Divine colors. Filled with Sacred song. May your daydreams become your days. May you drink from the purest waters. Stand beneath soft showers of sun. Nap in the down of clouds, light and free. May you remember your pristine composition, and not devalue it. May your true face emerge from seasons of doubt and fear, and may the catalog of your brilliance, your joy, your pricelessness, unfurl its pages, fluttering so lushly within your heart that you cannot help but cry. Completely. Utterly. Today. In Love. With this life. This miracle. This blessing. You are.

Superficial self-care on top of neglected self-Love can conceal unwellness and delay true healing. If we dig deeper and reach the roots of our suffering, if we touch those tendrils caringly, our ache becomes a poem. True self-care is an innate poem sung by the breath of self-Love. Self-Love is a fire we tend. Self-care is the heat that naturally arises to keep our soul supple and warm. Touch your heart more deeply every time. It will open and accommodate the depth of your healing Love.

Dear Softness, are you hard on yourself? If so, this behavior has roots. Were you treated harshly as a child? If so, this may be the root of you being hard on yourself. First, someone was hard on you. You figured they knew what they were doing, so you imitated!

Once you recognize this, you can begin to transform it. Let's say your objective is to learn how to be easy on yourself. Along the way, you will need to learn not to feel guilty about being easy on yourself. Through repeated ripples of gentleness in the way you touch your interior, being kind and tender comes to feel natural. One day, you pause and see how self-Loving you are, and how good it feels. Like freedom and safety. You realize being hard was never a life requirement. Now you are a presence of ease in the world that touches everything lightly. You are medicine. An endless springtime of beauty.

You may be walking through a very tender season of your life. Surely many seeds are being caressed by the way you walk. They will grow into a forest of blessings that will feed, comfort, and shelter many souls. Your grandmothers and grandfathers from the ages are with you. Their hands are on your shoulders. Water is in their eyes. Their hearts are swollen rivers filled with Love for you. They sing for you. Your soul is swaddled in their many blankets. You are safe, and a new sun rises inside to heal your wounds away. Drink when you thirst, dear one. Eat when you hunger. Rest when you tire. When you doubt, remember. Sing when you are lonesome. Dance when you grow restless. Be still, like the silent trees. Know that you are a divine thing, and already home.

Today, with all your dear heart, affirm yourself. Sanctify your relations. Hold ceremony with your soul. Let morning be a scripture, vast and uplifting. And the later hours a rhythm ladling peace. Grow silent enough to hear the trees growing, to feel the nascent publishing of hope in common lives. Dilate your spirit. Be a canyon. Filled with light. Let your dreams gather and drink. Yes, hold ceremony with your soul.

All my life living in the palace of my body, thinking it to be the palace of my soul. A new sun gleams the horizon today. I see now what all along Creation has been whispering to me in Love notes of breeze and sky. I am a soul. Which is my palace. And Grace, the keeper of all that lives there. Which includes my body. And when fear and pain visit my window, and I strain to hear Hope's music in the trees, a supple song I sing to myself, a song that stirs peace inside my sanctuary: *I am ordained in this season of my life*. Ordained in robes of change.

Goodness has bestowed upon me a single red blossom in the meadow of my wellness, a tender flower that needs to be touched and healed. The rosary of my life moments comforts me on my chest and in my hands. I polish its brilliant beads by remembering I am Loved. My whole life I have been feasting in the orchard of holy fortune. I am maiden to the River that knows me so well. Along those warm banks my Loved ones remain gathered, singing and crying and laughing with me. These are the days I tend the blossom in the meadow that needs my touch. I am not hostage within a long shade of misfortune. I am free and frolicking in the bright sun of circumstance. Even my tenderness is a celebration. My weariness rests itself into a resurrection of my life's vitality. Where I am uncertain in my being, Spirit shines the way.

Oh how I am remade in the womb of Providence. My soul is my palace. Eternity the countryside where my palace stands. I breakfast on fresh peace in the morning. Take my midday cups of serenity. I am Loved. I am Loved. I am in the meadow, nurturing the needful blossom inside of me. All that I feel is a string of notes in the music of Sacredness. Beauty has come to talk with me. I am in this, this moment I have been given to bathe my soul in uncertainty. Fate brings me close to the tall, wide window so I can breathe a blessed air and sunlight can touch me with its affection.

I am new in this journey. I am new in this amber meadow. I am new with each pulse of change, with every ache adorning my existence. Love is not my distant observer. Love is with me, in the spirit of all I Love and who Love me. Love is my sermon, my medicine, my giving rain. I am floating on an impossible sea of holiness, in waters that bear my weight. I am weightless. I am in this moment, already giving itself to the next moment whose water has broken, whose life is being born. My seasons have a sacred strategy. Soon I will have this moment as memory. And I will be new. New and singing all the notes of this life, my palatial life, rich of unforeseeable charity and fertile with fervent fields of Grace.

Every moment has its sunrise, sun peak, and sunset. Its expression of Sacred Will. When we learn to move in this supernatural harmony and rhythm, we are getting the most out of life. We are preciously squeezing our moments. Fresh juice is produced. When we learn to make deep use of these seeds planted in us, we become a forceful garden. Fruitful. Fulfilled.

Our life is not for our sake, but for the world's. The more efficient we are in harvesting what is planted in our moments, the more we have to share. The more plentiful our harvest, the more bountiful the meal of the masses. And in return, the more abundant our inner spring of Grace.

You are here, in this world, because you have been made to give. To open, part, and pour. To share, merge, and wed. To pollinate and flower. To increase the Light in all things. Keep learning your own way of moving inside the sunrise, sun peak, and sunset of your moments. This is how you grow your Peace.

There is an outer sun and an inner sun. We often seek the outer sun and grow dependent on the grace of weather. Neglecting our inner sun, which is always available, we grow unnecessarily dim and cold inside. Seeking to alleviate this suffering, we go on seeking the outer sun. Dear Soul, you need not be vacant of warmth and light. Sit with your innerness. Behold the candlelight you are growing, casting illumination on your corners and crevasses. Behold your soul thawing into dance. Behold the centerpiece of your central peace. Behold the sun you are.

Give yourself beautiful, sacred names each day. No need to restrict yourself. There are no rules in this. Claim the ones that make your soul sigh. Each name evokes a unique part of you. Particular notes in your song. Open the windows inside you. Let yourself out. Maybe we on earth aren't lacking self-Love. Maybe we lack sacred names. Self-Love lives in the names we call ourselves, and in the names we allow ourselves to be called. Time for a whole new language. One we can whisper in the hard moments to soften the soil. One we can lullaby ourselves to sleep with at night. Endless names exist whose sound and spirit feel good to your soul, for they are native to your soul. Claim them. Watch your life become a feel good thing.

Boundaries aren't walls that keep you in. They are windows that set you free. At first, you may feel guilty for not letting people take advantage of you any longer. As though their disappointment and hurt is more important than your wellness and freedom. Eventually you see the beauty and blessing in teaching people how you are to be treated. Those who care to honor this, stay. Those who never honored you to begin with go. What remains is a life in which you feel honored. Especially by yourself. Nothing feels freer than that. You will wish you had opened these windows to your sacredness long ago. For now, a modest first step. Say, *No*. Say it without guilt or apologies. Behold the life changing power of saying No to what does not feel good for you, and Yes to what feels right for you. You are conditioning yourself for peace. Now is a divine springtime of your life. Open your many windows. Breathe a fresher air.

A safe, free relationship space is like a wide open workshop for the soul. You can work on yourself there. We can spend many years in solitude "working on ourselves." And yet, solitude can blind us to certain growth needs, just as relationships of any kind can. The blessing of a healthy relationship, platonic or not, is to offer us a compassionate mirror for the soul. A nurturing, safe, reflective presence we can look into and see ourselves in ways we wouldn't otherwise. Two people, when practicing sacredness with each other and themselves, can create a beautiful space together, a tender garden where what trembles in them can be held and soothed until it grows bold and burgeoning into the sky.

The story you tell yourself about who you are is woven of a thousand threads of repetition. To heal and be free, unravel each thread patiently. Weave just as patiently the truth of your beautiful soul. Reweave you. Your idea of you, and therefore your life, is not an unchangeable stone. It is a weaving of rivers. A water that wants you to find the wonder in its waves. You are a creatable thing. Don't be afraid of the notes freedom sings.

When the world falls apart, you are blessed with a new window through which to see what truly matters. When the surreal becomes true life and the old illusions fall, take your opportunity to see what is real. Make that your life. Now is the time to gather your relations in spirit and Love. Light a fire. Talk story. Render beauty. Sacred blanket each other in goodness. Paint the night in a hopeful poetry. And when morning comes, no matter how difficult, soulrise into the world. Be a ceremony of compassion, a fountaining ambassador of Grace.

The world is not suddenly changing. It has always been changing. Its only nature is change. The appearance of consistency grants feelings of security. Many are privileged with this illusion of permanency. Eventually comes a moment that lifts the veil. This is that moment. Now is a season to breathe deeply into this opportunity to see life as it is: continuous transformation.

Breathing is valuable when moving through change. Breathing is a release valve for anxiety, a multidirectional passage for peace. May we hold one another in beautiful breathing, according to our own capacity. May we hold each other in the priceless energy of caring. May we feed our docile inclinations for kindness, along inward and outward planes.

Notice how the sun still rises, the sky still stretches. Earth yet beds our personal and collective being. All that is good in you is good in you beyond condition. All that you hope for is already here. You may not recognize it, for gifts often wear clothes we do not anticipate. They do not hew to trend or style. Today, may you set your eyes toward these modest blessings. May you softly look past their sometimes dreary, threatening outer wardrobe and see the naked glory they bring to living things. We say, Peace be with you. Grace be with you. All the Love and language of life, sweet life, be with you. This is not a prayer. This is testimony of truth. These gifts *be* with you.

It is time for each of us to determine what medicine we have to offer the world. Concerned only for yourself, you fall into despair. Concerned only for your people, you fall into delusion. But when you offer who you are, what you have, to the world, you rise into purpose fulfilled. You rise into unconditional peace. What are your sacred medicines? Surely you overflow with the nectar of your own particular Grace. Find that, and give it. In your giving you lose your fear, anxiety, confusion, loneliness. Give your goodness. You shall be revealed. You shall be healed.

Do not worry whether the glass is half full or half empty. Concern yourself with what is in the glass. What purpose is in the glass of this moment, dear soul? That is the question. Breathe beautifully and contemplate what this moment means for you. For the world. Filled with Grace, begin planting. This is a planting season. Soon the glorious harvest. What are your divine crops?

Love like the sincerity of sunlight. Absolute. Pure. Unrestrained and unobstructed. Without strategy, motive, or doubt. Love like this, naked and obliterated, shorn of every sheath and veil, nude to all that bears witness, and you too can power an entire world. Sincerity penetrates us. If you wish to deliver your medicine deep into the human heart, be sincere.

Like the candor of Love,
sincerity of sunlight,
incense of memory,
this era on earth
of your soul.

If this book touched you, you can touch it back.

Please consider writing an **online reader review** at Amazon, Barnes & Noble, or Goodreads. Reviews are a valuable way to support the life of a book and especially to support an independent author.

Freely **post social media photos** of you or others with the book, just the book itself, or passages from the book. Please kindly include the hashtag **#JAIYAJOHN.**

I cherish your support of my books and our Soul Water Rising rehumanizing mission around the world.

BOOK ANGEL PROJECT

Your book purchases support our global *Book Angel Project,* which provides scholarships and book donations for vulnerable youth, and places gift copies of my inspirational books throughout communities worldwide, to be discovered by the souls who need them. The books are left in places where hearts are tender: hospitals, nursing homes, prisons, wellness centers, group homes, mental health clinics, and other community spaces.

If you are fortunate to discover one of our *Book Angel* gift books, please kindly post a photo of you with the book on Instagram, using the hashtag **#JAIYAJOHN**, or email it to us at **books@soulwater.org**. Thank you!

I Will Read for You:
The Voice and Writings of Jaiya John

A podcast. Voice medicine to soothe your soul, from poet, author, and spoken word artist Jaiya John. Bedtime bliss. Morning meditation. Daytime peace. Comfort. Calm. Soul food. Come, gather around the fire. Let me read for you. **Spotify. Apple. Wherever podcasts roam.**

Dr. Jaiya John shares freedom work and healing messages with audiences worldwide. He was orphan-born on Ancient Puebloan lands in the desert of New Mexico, is a former professor of social psychology at Howard University, and has lived in various locations, including Kathmandu, Nepal. Jaiya is the author of numerous books, and the founder of Soul Water Rising, a global rehumanizing mission supporting the healing and wholeness of vulnerable and oppressed populations.

Jacqueline V. Carter and Kent W. Mortensen served graciously, faithfully, and skillfully as editors for *Freedom*. I am forever grateful for their Love labor.

Secure a Jaiya John keynote or talk:

jaiyajohn.com

OTHER BOOKS BY JAIYA JOHN

Jaiya John titles are available online where books are sold. To learn more about this and other books by Jaiya, to order **discounted bulk quantities**, and to learn about Soul Water Rising's global freedom work, please visit us at:

jaiyajohn.com

books@soulwater.org

@jaiyajohn (IG FB TW YT)